FERNITICKLES

Written by Mary Peace Finley
Illustrated by Anita Vink

© 1995 Shortland Publications Inc.

03 02 01 00 99 98
11 10 9 8 7 6 5 4 3

Published by Shortland Publications Inc.
Produced by Shortland Publications,
2B Cawley Street, Ellerslie, Auckland, New Zealand.

Distributed in the United States of America by

a division of Reed Elsevier Inc.
500 Coventry Lane
Crystal Lake, IL 60014
800-822-8661

Distributed in Canada by

PRENTICE HALL GINN
1870 Birchmount Road
Scarborough
Ontario M1P 2J7

Printed through Bookbuilders Limited, Hong Kong.

ISBN: 0-7901-0999-9

CONTENTS

CHAPTER 1

Duncan Fisher slipped a piece of smoked salmon and a barley bannock into the leather bag at his waist. Smiling, he looked through the open window of his house, past the town of Stirling, toward Stirling Castle. For fourteen years, since three years before Duncan's birth, Stirling Castle had stood empty on a black stone crag above the town, waiting for the King's promised return. Today the King was coming home.

The people of Stirling had long prepared for the King. They passed laws to stop poaching in King's Park. They repaired the city gate and the road. They gathered tapestries and robes and silver vessels from all over Scotland. They gilded His

Majesty's coat of arms and the cross at the Tollbooth with gold.

With the King's return, the people of Stirling once again dared to dream of riches and fame. On this early summer day in the year 1617, that dream flickered from one to another like a smile.

But Duncan's smile was not for gold, and it was not for the King. Duncan smiled because no one would work today. Even Duncan and his father, John Fisher, the Village Fisher, would not fish until after King James arrived. Duncan could watch his otters.

"I'll be going now." He ducked under the carved wooden fish that hung above the doorway of his family's stone and wood house.

"Aye, no ye wil'na, lad!" A rough hand grasped his arm. "Ye wil'na be going to the river today, and ye wil'na be playing the fool with the wild creatures of the woods! Today we honor our returning King."

Duncan knew his father would never understand. He could not tell him about the months of waiting or his weeks of gentle coaxing. He could not tell him what the otters had done just yesterday. For John Fisher, otters meant only two things: torn nets and pilfered fish. "But father,"

Duncan said, "why should I honor King James? He has been in England since before I was born!" Duncan eased away from his father's grip. "Uncle William says Scotland is better off without him. We Scots don't need an English king to tell us what to do!"

"James the First is *not* an English King!" John Fisher's face grew red. "James the First is the first King of Scotland to be King of England, too!"

"That is not what Uncle William says. Uncle William says James is English through and through. Uncle William says the King is just a salmon, swimming upriver to where he was spawned."

"Och! Duncan! Duncan, lad, ye listen to my baby brother too much. William talks too much with these reformers! He is too young to remember." Rubbing his rough hands together, Duncan's father sighed. Then he smiled the way he always did when he looked into the past. "Aye! Those days when the royal court was at Stirling Castle, Stirling was a true royal burgh. It bustled with court visitors and trade. Aye, those were fine, wonderful days."

"Fine, wonderful days, indeed!" Duncan's mother, Ishbel, rushed from the house and thrust a package into Duncan's hands. Her hair was uncovered and still uncombed, and her eyes were tired looking and red. "Finished, and just in time. Duncan, run and deliver this gown for the wee bairn of the Earl of Mar. Hurry, before the King's procession arrives."

"I will, Mother." Duncan took the package – and the opportunity to escape. "But, Mother, the Earl should not ha' asked you to knit this in only one day's time. You've worked all night."

"No, he should not have." Duncan's mother reached behind her and pulled Duncan's little sister, Fiona, from the folds of her skirt where she was hiding. "I think your father has forgotten. That was the way of those 'fine, wonderful days' of 'More!' and 'Now!'"

John's droopy mustache flared. His eyes shot from his wife, over the golden hair of his daughter, and riveted on Duncan. "King James will bring new hope, even for a fisher's son! Ye will see!" He grabbed his pipe and stomped away.

CHAPTER 2

Clutching his mother's package, Duncan skirted a leper hobbling down the street toward the river. Lepers were not supposed to be seen today. "Me neither," Duncan whispered. He could already hear the skirl of bagpipes and the rattle of drums. The royal procession was approaching. He would have to hurry.

Duncan climbed the steep road that led up from the flat, boggy carseland. Behind him, the Water of Forth meandered eastward like a great snake. It looped its way through the wide valley toward the Firth of Forth and into the North Sea. In front of him, on top of a great dolerite pinnacle, loomed Stirling Castle. The town of Stirling perched on the steep slope in between.

"Duncan! Wait!" Fiona was panting up the street behind him, holding her skirts high.

"Fiona, you canna' tag along. Not this time!"

"But I want…"

"Fiona! Go back home. I won't be coming back. I canna' miss the otters today, not for anything, not even the King." Duncan stooped and whispered into the soft hair around Fiona's ear. "Nosey touched me yesterday!"

"Ohhh!" Fiona's blue eyes stretched wide. "The one with the pink nose?"

"Aye! Now go. Bow to the King for me."

The cornets sounded. Duncan straightened up. Glancing over his shoulder, he hurried up St. Mary's Wynd. He rushed past women and little girls in sun-bleached linen aprons holding flowers. He ran past men and boys proudly standing before their freshly tidied stalls. Everything was ready. After the mist and rain of the day before, the Water of Forth and the blue Scottish sky sparkled as if they, too, had been scrubbed for the King's return.

"If the King likes my boots," the Cobbler was saying to his wife as Duncan passed, "perhaps he will..." His words stopped midsentence. "Duncan, where are ye going, lad? Stand here with us. The King will be coming soon."

"No, thank you," Duncan called over his shoulder. "I must deliver this gown for the wee bairn of the Earl of Mar. Mother worked all night..."

Johnne Anderson, the Baxter, was balancing a steaming pile of fluffy scones on a large wooden platter. Smiling down at his children, he said, "If the King fancies our loaves and scones..." As the Baxter glanced up, the smile slid down his face. "Duncan! Whatever are ye doing? Get that heap of red hair over here, out of the path of the King."

Rich smells of scones and apples and a glimpse of Lillias, the Baxter's daughter, tempted Duncan to stop. But he ran on, right up the crown of the road. Only the King and nobility were supposed to use these raised center stones. Everybody knew that. But today, Duncan ran there anyway. He didn't want the sewage and filth that ran down the sides of the streets to splash on the new gown.

"Duncan," the Baxter called again. "Come over here, lad!"

"No, thank you." Duncan waved to the Baxter's family and to the men gathered outside Janet Kilbowie's tavern holding mugs of ale. The Innkeeper was leaning back, wiping her hands on her skirt and saying, "If he does, I could be named the Royal Maltster."

"And I, the Royal Cheesemaker!" Duncan saw his uncle, Charles Fisher, toasting himself with an enormous round of cheese in one pudgy hand and a mug of ale in the other.

"And I, the Royal Huntsman," roared the tall man covered in green leather from the toes of his boots to the tip of his huntsman's cap. He swept a crossbow and arrow from his back and, squinting, pretended to take aim.

"And I…" With a flourish, the pumpkin-shaped fellow next to him flung the pelt of a red fox around his neck. "The Royal Furrier!" He posed like a nobleman, with his long, tapered fingertips touching together.

At the sight of the pelt, Duncan shivered, but excited voices swept away the sad memory of his red-furred friend. Behind him, out of sight around a bend, the drone of pipes and drums stopped.

Silence chilled the air; then a cornet blared the royal fanfare. For the first time in Duncan's life, the King and his royal entourage entered the royal burgh of Stirling.

Duncan raced toward the Earl of Mar's three-story house at the top of Broad Street. He ran past the Mercat Cross, where the market was held. He ran past the Tron, where goods were weighed, and past the Tollbooth, where the assembled town fathers stood waiting. Only Uncle William's friend, Patrik Sympsone, the Minister of the Rude Kirk of Stirling, looked glum. The Town Bellman, the Town Drummer, and the Burgh Piper were smiling. Their bells and drums and bagpipes were ready. Robert Murray, greeting speech in hand, glowered at Duncan. The Burgh Executioner shook a clenched fist and yelled, "Get ye gone, or I will throw that freckly face in the brig!"

The beat of the drums grew louder. Closer. Duncan lunged toward the house at the top of the town and pounded on the heavy door. "Here!" He thrust the baby gown into the hands of a servant.

Behind him, the hooves of prancing horses tapped like cobblers' hammers on the cobblestone street. Looking for a way to escape, Duncan darted toward the entrance of Hangman's Close. Tom the Tinker's horse and wagon were hitched there, blocking the way. When Duncan turned back, it was too late.

Like an army, the King's procession was advancing. Even though Duncan was at the other end of the street, he could feel the power of the King's eyes on him.

Slowly, he turned to face the King. He bowed low, one knee to the ground. Alone on the crown of Broad Street, Duncan held his breath, trembling. Afraid to look up, he stared down at a round piece of tin. When he felt the King look away, Duncan scooped up the tin button and fled.

CHAPTER 3

Duncan ran up toward the castle. He darted behind the Kirk, zigzagged through the cemetery, and plunged down the steep path on the far side of Stirling Castle.

At the base of the pinnacle, he leaned against the cold stone, out of breath. From this side, the castle loomed straight above him. The pipes and drums sounded far away. No one would see him here, but to be safe, he would go to his otters along a path hidden in the woods of Gowan Hills.

Those woods held danger. Wild boars and ferocious white cows lived there. But Duncan was always careful. He was not afraid to be in the woods alone.

The woods of Gowan Hills were dark. Few sun

spots found their way through the roof of leaves overhead. The air was damp and cool and smelled of decaying leaves.

Duncan knew the path well. He knew all the paths and trails and roads around Stirling, and he knew other secret ways, besides the old Roman causeway, to cross the boggy carseland. Although the path was knobby with tree roots, Duncan darted along, as swift and surefooted as the wild forest animals that lived there. Two large doves fluttered up from the underbrush. Their wings clattered against the thick leaves of the trees. This had been the home of the red fox. She had been the first of the forest animals to let him come near. Now she was a neck piece for the Furrier.

Brushing his sadness aside, Duncan paused at the edge of the woods and looked out across the marshy plain. He could hear a faint swish of water, and from the distance, the cornets echoing down from the crag. Yesterday the otters were upriver from the Stirling Bridge and the harbor. He would look there again. Crouching, he eased toward the river, watching for otters.

"Chi! Chichichichi!" Duncan called, imitating

the cry that meant 'Here I am. Where are you?' "Chi! Chichichichi!"

A startled red deer leapt up from its bed and thundered into the woods. Wild geese rose from the water, honking. Then it became quiet again.

"Chi! Chi!" The sleek brown otter was twice the size of a mink. It loped along an otter trail through the grass and splashed into the Forth.

"Nosey? Is that you?"

Duncan slid, stomach down, onto the bank and peered through the long blades of grass and curly leafed ferns. "Only one otter today." He didn't think it was Nosey. She was never alone.

For weeks, the otters had scampered away whenever Duncan came. Nosey and Grilse were still babies then. Mother Otter would not let anyone come near, not even their father. Now that Nosey and Grilse were almost as large as their mother, the whole family sometimes romped and played together.

"Chi!" Duncan chirped, scanning the water. "Where did you go?" A pair of white swans glided by on the river, looking his way, but the otter had disappeared.

About a month ago, Mother Otter and the two cubs stopped their play and stared at the place where Duncan was hiding. They sniffed the air. They chittered and chattered and whistled at him, then, almost with a shrug, went back to their game. They didn't run away. Since then, little by little, day by day, Duncan eased closer and closer. He watched them play like little clowns, rolling and tumbling over one another. They dived for bright pebbles on the riverbed and rode the ripples where the current was fast. They wrestled and chased each other and played hide-and-seek – just for fun. Sometimes they rubbed noses.

"Chi!" Duncan chirped. The otter was scrambling out of the water several yards downriver. It was three or four feet long, as big as Uncle Charles' sheepdogs. Its fur parted in drippy V-shaped clumps. It shook itself so vigorously that it slid backward into the river.

Laughing, Duncan slipped his fingers into the Water of Forth. "The whole burgh of Stirling and all the sailors at Stirling Harbor can watch the King if they like. I'd rather be right here watching otters. If I could, I'd spend my whole life watching otters."

Duncan called again, "Chi! Chichichichi!"

With a splash, the otter bobbed up like a cork, holding its paws in front of its chest, and chirped back.

"Chiiirp!" Duncan answered. "Oh, it's you, Father Otter." Father Otter was larger and darker than the

others, and had a funny curlicue on the edge of his left ear. "Where's the rest of your family today?"

Father Otter rolled over in the water, dived, then popped up closer to shore.

Duncan lay on the bank, remembering too late not to get grass stains on his new white shirt or

brown hose. He reached into his pocket for the tinker's button he'd found in the street. "Here!" He tossed the tin button into the air and caught it again. Father Otter's bright black eyes followed the button. "This is for you." The tin glimmered as it sailed through the air and plopped into the river.

With a flip, Father Otter submerged, then surfaced with the button clasped between his front paws. He snorted loudly, blowing water from his nose. Duncan was sure he saw a smile on Father Otter's face.

"Do you like that button, Father Otter? Good! Now, bring it here!" Duncan knew the otter wouldn't understand, but he held out his hand anyway. "Bring it here, Father Otter. Bring me the button."

The otter slithered under the stream bank out of sight.

The fanfare was now coming from high on the promontory – a sign that the procession would soon be over. In the village, work would begin again. Duncan scanned the water and along the bank, but Father Otter was nowhere to be seen. "I'll be back," Duncan called, "as soon as I can."

He jumped up and ran back toward the town. He could see the King's banners waving high on the road entering the castle. The townspeople were turning toward home. His father would be one of them.

Duncan knew that many people in Stirling were happy today. The King had come, they said, because returning to Scotland would make him feel young again. He had come because of the abundance of fish in the waters and game in the woods, and because he loved to hunt where he had hunted as a boy. He had come because of the fine quality of the local cheeses and ales.

But as Duncan hurried over the muddy path toward home, he wondered about Uncle William and all the people who were not happy with King James's return. Nobody had mentioned how hard it would be to provide fish and meat and rolls and cheese for all the royal entourage. And nobody had asked why the King had left the castles where he'd lived before.

CHAPTER 4

"Duncan!" Duncan knew his father was never as gruff as he sounded. Duncan turned toward the voice and the faint smell of fish and tobacco and freshly carved wood. As his eyes adjusted to the dark interior of their home, he bit his lip to hide a smile. His father's squat face and droopy, white whiskers looked just like Father Otter's.

John Fisher thumped his carving onto the table and squinted up at Duncan. He grumbled around the pipe he held clenched between his teeth. "Fiona tells me ye were in the forest with those worthless otters again!"

Again? Had Father known all along?

"Duncan, lad, ye should ha' been here to greet the King! He is the King, Duncan, God's appointed one." His father's hands dropped to his knees and a flurry of shavings drifted to the floor. "Son," his voice mellowed, "listen to me, lad. We are simple people. 'Tis our lot to work hard until good fortune smiles on us. And good fortune is smiling today. Before ye were born, lad, before the King left for England, he made many special appointments..."

Interrupted by a loud knock on the open door, Duncan's father jumped to his feet. He jerked the pipe from between his teeth. His three-legged stool clattered to its side. Duncan turned. In the doorway stood a lad a little taller than himself. He was wearing a flat hat with a tall feather on top, tight-fitting blue hose, and an embroidered tunic. Behind him stood a large draft horse hitched to a cart loaded with baskets.

"Excuse me," the boy said in a strong English accent and more loudly than was necessary. "I am Myron, Messenger for the King."

"Och! Aye!" Duncan's father sputtered. "Please do come in."

"Thank you, but I am here only to order fish for the King. That is, if you are John Fisher, Fisher of this royal burgh."

"Indeed! The very same." John Fisher rubbed a stubby finger across his bushy eyebrow. "And this is my son and very fine helper, Duncan. Duncan Fisher." He turned to Duncan's mother, who sat spinning in the far corner of the room near the chimney. "Ishbel, my wife, and…"

But the messenger's eyes had not left Duncan. "Ah, yes. I know who you are," he interrupted. A smile flickered across his face. "What is it you Scots say for 'freckles'? Ah, yes! Fernitickles! Fernitickles, the boy who ran from the King. The King finds you most interesting."

"But I…" Duncan's throat squeezed shut. "I didn't run from the King!" And I *hate* being called Fernitickles, he thought.

"Never mind," the messenger said, flipping his hand as if to brush the thought away. "Our King is a good King, very wise and slow to anger. But it is true that he is quite particular. He must have fresh fish for his table. It is, in part, because of the sparkling water of Forth – and fresh fish – that the King has returned. Tomorrow, for the evening meal, after his game of golf, the King orders you to catch fifty fish. I shall come for them in the late afternoon."

"Good! Very good!" Duncan's father bowed. "The fish will be ready. And they will be fresh."

As the messenger led his packhorse toward the bakery and cheese stalls, Duncan's father turned to Duncan and Ishbel and Fiona. His blue eyes sparkled even more than usual. "Oh, this is good. This is very good. What did I tell you?" He rubbed his hands together. "Such a big order! In the morning, Duncan, I'll leave ye to fish above the bridge while I fish from the boat below the bridge. And Ishbel, my love, ye best tie us a new net. A large one for the boat. We may be needing it soon."

"Duncan?" Fiona pirouetted across the room, daintily holding up the hem of her apron. "Isn't the King's messenger handsome?"

"I didn't notice, little Princess Tattletale." Duncan bowed low, then spun her around whispering, "But I did notice that this English messenger may ha' brought me a royal lot of trouble."

CHAPTER 5

Duncan was in the woods so early the next morning that the first birdsongs were still rustling from the leaves. A startled doe looked up at him from where she was browsing on newly sprouted grass. A black polecat with a white stripe swished across the path, and squirrels scolded as they scrambled up and down tree trunks. Duncan spoke to them all, and laughed at the long-eared conies hopping and hunching everywhere. He saw paw prints of other animals that had passed in the night – a wildcat, a fox, and a hedgehog. Early morning was his favorite time of day, when the daytime animals were waking and the nighttime animals had just gone to bed. He hoped to spot his otters soon. Morning was their favorite time to play.

The last thing his father had called from the boat was, "Now mind ye, Duncan, a man canna' always do what he'druther. Today I canna' be whittling, and ye canna' be fooling with otters."

Duncan carried a net, fish bags, his cleaning knife, and a three-pronged gaff. He would fish. Even though he didn't like fishing any more than his father did, they were both good fishermen. But, Duncan thought, as long as I catch what we need, I don't see any harm in fishing where I can watch the otters, too.

He'd learned that his otters traveled fast and far, sometimes northeast to the Allan Water, and sometimes far downriver toward the Firth of Forth. He wondered if they ever went out into the North Sea. This morning they weren't anywhere near the harbor where he helped his father launch the flat-bottomed fishing boat. There was no sign of them where he'd seen Father Otter yesterday, except for the occasional places where the otters returned again and again to drop their scat and leave their scent.

"Chi?" Duncan called.

No answer.

He wandered on, and soon found a place where the otters had rolled, bending down the fresh, green blades of grass. Next he came to a freshly scuffed area where they had squirmed and wallowed in a dirt bath. He rounded a large bend in the Forth and crossed over a small rise. There they were, all four of them, fishing for their breakfast.

Like miniature sea serpents, they plowed through the water and dived. Duncan could only imagine the underwater chase. When they surfaced, each one clasped a fat trout or an eel wriggling between sharp teeth. Each one except Grilse. As usual, Grilse came up with his own favorite delicacy – a grilse, a young salmon on its first return up the Forth from the sea.

The otters are wise, Duncan thought, as the edges of his small net slipped through his fingers. They know the perfect place to fish.

By midmorning, the fish bags were so full they threatened to tear apart. Duncan had caught and cleaned fifty salmon, and two more for good measure. That was many more than he would usually have caught in such a short time. If his

father also had good luck, there would be fish for the King and all the townspeople, too. Duncan sank the bags into the cold water in the shade of the bank to keep his catch fresh for the King's table. Then he ate an early lunch of hard cheese and bread and lay down beside the river.

"Chi! Chichichichichi!" he called, wishing he had another tin button. After their early morning antics, the otters had disappeared. "Chi! Chichichi!"

Mallards had waddled ashore and tucked their heads under their wings for a midday rest. Even the herons, standing as still as dead twigs at the edge of the water, looked asleep. Duncan suspected that the otters were napping, too, in an otter holt upwind of him by the river.

"Chi! Chichichichi!"

"Chirp!" Like four rollicking puppies, the otters bounded, humpbacked and sleepy eyed, through the grass toward him, then stopped short. They blinked and stared and sniffed the air. Duncan knew they couldn't see very well. He lay perfectly still.

"Chirp!" Nosey came closer, but Mother Otter grunted, and the cub froze. Then, apparently forgetting all about him, all four – Mother, Father, Nosey, and Grilse – tumbled into the river to play.

Slowly, Duncan slid his hand into the ice-cold water and wiggled his fingers. If the otters mistook him for something to eat, he could get a nasty bite, but it was worth the risk. If they got used to his fingers, then his hand, then his arm in the water, maybe they'd let him swim with them.

He dangled his hand underwater for so long it became numb. He was about to take it out when a nose bumped the ends of his fingers. Father Otter popped up out of the water and blinked.

"Chi!" Duncan said.

"Chi!" Father Otter answered, then wriggled onto the bank, planted his front paws, and shook like a dog. Water flipped from his loose, thick fur into Duncan's face and over his clothes.

"Hey!" Duncan yelped. Father Otter plunged back into the river.

Duncan's heart was racing. Father Otter had come so close! He had answered. Yesterday he had taken his button, and the day before, Nosey had touched him with her nose. A shiver tingled through Duncan's scalp. This was the time to find out. Would they let him into their world? Would they let him swim with them?

Quickly Duncan glanced about. Seeing no one, he jerked his shirt over his head. He flung his hose aside, and naked, stood for a second on the bank and braced himself for the shock of cold. He dived.

Underwater, he opened his eyes. Everything was greenish blue and dappled with shadow. He couldn't see where the otters had gone. Finally, out of breath, he surfaced.

Just as he did, splat! Grilse hit the water with a loud splash. Now Nosey was sailing down a long, muddy slide. Her front paws were tucked to her sides. She held her chin high, like a little girl sledding on snow. Splat! She hit the water.

Duncan ducked underwater and watched. A churning mass of bubbles and mud swirled around the wiggling otter as she swooped toward him. Her eyes were open, ears plastered close against her head, tail pumping from side to side. Like a falcon in flight, she circled around him to return to the bank. Then she scrambled up the edge of the muddy slide for another turn.

Splat!

Splat!

Splat! One after another, the otters slid down the mud and belly flopped into the river. "You funny otters!" Duncan laughed. This was more wonderful than he'd ever imagined. He was swimming with otters! "Do you think I'm an otter with no fur? Well," he called out, paddling toward the mud slide, "if I'm one of you, then it's my turn!"

Duncan hoisted himself up and scrambled to the top of the muddy bank. At the top, Father Otter scurried in frantic circles. He peered at Duncan with a look that could have been his own father's, a look that on the surface was grumpy, but kind.

Duncan laughed. "I know. I'm mad!" He lay belly down in the slippery mud and pushed off, careening down toward the river. Just before he hit the surface, he glanced up. Myron, the King's messenger, was standing by Duncan's discarded clothes. He was waving his flat hat and yelling something that was lost as Duncan's ears were deafened by gurgling water.

CHAPTER 6

Duncan wanted to stay underwater forever. If he could, he would change himself into an otter that Myron wouldn't recognize. But eventually, he had to come up for air.

Myron was leaning over the bank. "Fernitickles!" he shouted. "Why aren't you fishing?"

Duncan huddled low in the water as Myron's words pelted him from the shore.

"The King has changed his royal mind. He must have the fish for luncheon instead of dinner. Your father is still fishing from the boat below the bridge. He is too far out to hear me. Your mother sent me to find you." He glanced up at the sun, which was nearly overhead. "And I find you, playing

like a child! Oh, we shall both be in terrible trouble! And so shall your father."

"But – but…" Duncan spluttered. "I was…" He turned to point at the otters, to explain. But the otters were now nowhere to be seen. What a fool he must seem. "I have the fish," he said softly.

"You have the fish?" Myron's head jerked to the right, then to the left. "Where? All fifty of them?"

Trying to keep his body underwater and out of

sight, Duncan paddled to the bags of fish. He couldn't reach the ties. "Ah, Myron," he called, "could you help?"

The worried look left Myron's face when he saw the heavy bags of salmon Duncan was struggling to hoist from the river. "Oh! These are beautiful, Fernitickles! The King will be pleased." Myron's eyes twinkled as he dumped the catch into the baskets on his horse cart. For a moment he looked as if he'd forgotten he was the Royal Messenger. "Fernitickles, you're so muddy, I can't see your freckles! Do you do that often? Slide in mud?"

Duncan grinned and tried to think of something to say.

"Never mind. I must hurry." Myron flipped his hand as if to brush the question away. Like a mask, the Royal Messenger expression clamped back onto his face. "Tomorrow, the King will host a royal banquet. Tell your father the King will need one hundred and fifty fresh fish. I shall come for them late in the afternoon. Remember, our King is a good King, very wise and slow to anger, but he does expect the very freshest fish."

As soon as Myron was out of sight, Duncan scrambled out of the pool and jumped into his clothes. With a final "chirp" at his traitorous otters, he ran home. An order for one hundred and fifty fish was the largest he and his father had ever had. He wondered how they could possibly catch that many.

CHAPTER 7

"John Fisher! Duncan!" The Baxter and his daughter, Lillias, ran into the street, waving. "Such news! The King fancied our breads! What did I tell you? The King will make us rich. Now he has ordered three hundred rolls baked in the shape of his crown." Chuckling, the Baxter brushed flour from his apron. "Lillias and the other children will help. We must begin well before dawn."

"So must we." John Fisher pointed his pipe toward the river. "One hundred and fifty fresh fish the King wants! Imagine! We've never netted that many in a single day. 'Tis a good thing we have the extra fish I caught today. But if the King wants them early again tomorrow..." He shook his head. "Only the kindness of providence gave Duncan such good luck this time."

"And the kindness of the otters," Duncan said, trying to catch Lillias's eye. Immediately he regretted his words. "I mean," he ducked, glancing toward his father, "the otters showed me a deep hole where the good fishing was."

John Fisher's face clouded over like the sky in a storm. "And the otters are there," he thundered, "because they catch fish! Our fish! Otters! They eat our fish. They tear our nets. They're nothing but a nuisance!" He turned to the Baxter. "Do they give milk like cows?"

"No." The Baxter chuckled.

"Do they give eggs like hens?" He aimed his pipe at Lillias and furrowed his bushy eyebrows.

"No," she answered, but her voice was soft, and she glanced apologetically toward Duncan.

"Can ye ride them like horses? No! I tell ye, Duncan, stay away from otters. They're nothing but trouble. There's only one good use for otters…"

Duncan knew what his father was going to say. "Aren't they good for just being themselves?" he interrupted.

His father's eyebrows danced a little jig on his

forehead. He turned to the Baxter and shrugged. "What an odd thing to say."

Duncan and Lillias and their fathers joined the throng of townspeople. Everyone crowded into Janet Kilbowie's tavern, toasting their good fortune. Duncan's Uncle Charles cheered the King's order for ten great rounds of cheese. The Innkeeper had already hired a woodcarver to chisel a sign proclaiming herself "The King's Royal Maltster." Now she passed free mugs of ale to the adults and apple juice to the children. Duncan took a mug, then squeezed through the crowd to stand next to Lillias. "The otters let me swim with them today!" he whispered.

The Innkeeper raised her mug and her voice. "To King James! Long live the King!"

Everyone, except Uncle William and his crowd of friends standing near the door, chimed in. "Long live the King!"

From outside, the Huntsman's bugle drowned out the Innkeeper's toast. The Huntsman bounded into the tavern. "Good news!" he shouted. "The King has commissioned me to hunt hart and hare for the royal banquet."

"And good news for us both!" The long, tapered fingers of the Furrier waved in the air above the Huntsman's shoulder. He hopped up and down to be seen. "The King has ordered me to make two fine winter cloaks, one for the Queen's birthday, and the other for the Lady Rebekah – whoever she may be."

"Why, you're in doubly good luck, then!" Lillias's father exclaimed, raising his cup. "Duncan! Tell the Huntsman where ye saw those otters. There'd be no finer cloak for the Queen than one made from the pelts of otters."

The juice rolling over Duncan's tongue whistled down his windpipe and peppered his lungs. Choking, he gasped for breath, then doubled over in a fit of coughing.

"Duncan!" His father pounded his back. "Lad, are ye all right? Duncan?"

But Duncan was unable to speak.

CHAPTER 8

The following morning, Duncan was on the forest trail at the crack of dawn. Ghostly white mist swirled through the trees, touching his face and neck with pinpoints of moisture. In the semidarkness, night creatures scuttled through the leaves like whispers. An unseen owl hooted in a tree, and farther away, another owlet answered. During the night, Duncan had hardly slept at all. Each time he closed his eyes, he saw the glee on the Furrier's face when Lillias's father told him about the otters.

Duncan found the otter family working as a team this morning, as happy in fog as in sunshine. They were herding fish into the shallows below a deep pool, making it easier to catch their breakfast. The dark shadows of salmon fled before

Mother and Father Otter into the trap. Then Nosey and Grilse darted in for the kill.

"Go! Go away!" Duncan shouted. He ran toward the stream, tossing handfuls of pebbles at them.

"Chirp!" Grilse pulled a fish onto a rock, swiftly chewed off its fins so it wouldn't escape, then dived after one of the pebbles.

"No! No! No! Go away!" Duncan yelled again, flailing his arms. "All of you! Escape to the highlands. Go out to sea! Go far away, or you'll be caught as easily as you caught that fish!"

Grilse surfaced with a pebble and dropped it on the bank, then tipped his head. His bright pink tongue protruded comically from between his teeth.

"Go!" Duncan shouted. "Go! Don't you get it? You aren't safe here! This is no game!"

But Grilse ran in playful circles, and Nosey and Mother Otter wiggled up the bank to join him. Nosey was carrying something round clasped between her teeth.

"Nosey! Where did you get that?" It was a round leather golf ball – probably one of the King's. Feathers were sticking out of the holes punctured by the otter's teeth.

Any other time, Duncan would have laughed. He would have played catch or fetch, but now Duncan growled and grunted and hissed. He waved his arms. "If you don't want to be a cloak for the Queen, then go! Shoo! Go!" But they didn't go. Duncan jerked Nosey's golf ball from her mouth and flung it into the pool. "Now, go!"

Nosey dived after it, and in no time at all, returned. Smiling up at Duncan, she placed the ball at his feet.

"Oh, this is terrible," Duncan groaned, sinking to the ground. "And it's all my fault the Huntsman knows you're here. If only I hadn't been trying to impress Lillias…"

It took Duncan all day to catch thirty-nine salmon, and in spite of his yelling and growling, the otters wouldn't go away. They rolled and tumbled and dived and slid as if all his warnings were play. A light rain was falling, making him clammy and cold. Feeling miserable, Duncan lugged his catch back home along the path, hoping that his father's luck had been better. He hoped that the Huntsman was still too busy hunting meat for the banquet to be looking for otters.

When he ducked into the little cottage, into the warm smell of burning peat and gorse, Duncan knew there was trouble.

Without so much as a greeting, his father sprang to his feet, gripping his knife in one hand and a block of wood in the other. "How many?"

"Thirty-nine."

John Fisher sank back onto his stool. "And I, only fifty-three."

"What else can ye do, then?" Ishbel's hands stopped knitting.

Duncan's father shook his head. "Nothing, my love." Slowly, he bent again over his carving. Three large slivers of birch curled from the blade of his knife and floated, silent as snow, to the floor. "Nothing."

When Myron arrived, John and Duncan delivered one hundred and fifty fish, ninety-two of which were fresh. The other fifty-eight were caught yesterday.

"The King was very pleased with the fish." Myron smiled broadly. He dropped one gold ducat, a half merk, and twopence into John's hand. Fiona peeked from behind her mother's skirt, not taking her eyes from the messenger. "'The fish were very fresh,' the King says to tell you. And," Myron's smile was genuine, "the King hinted that an even greater reward may soon come your way. Our King is a good King, very wise and slow to anger," Myron laughed. "But he does like his fish fresh."

Duncan saw the Adam's apple lift and fall in his father's throat. "We are honored that the King was pleased," John Fisher said; but his voice went from gruff to soft and back to gruff again, out of control.

"And good news! The King and his guests enjoyed your catch so much that for tomorrow," Myron announced, with a flourish of his hat, "the court will need two hundred and twenty-five more!"

Duncan felt as if something hard had hit him in the stomach. He couldn't breathe. "But – but…" he stammered.

"Duncan." His father held up his hand. "We must try."

Myron tilted his head. His smile faded. "If it is too difficult for you, perhaps the King will send some of his men to help."

"Oh, no! No! No!" John Fisher's whiskers fanned stiffly from his lip. "We wilna' be needing any help."

"Very well, then." As he left, Myron glanced back at Duncan and winked. "Beware of muddy banks!"

Duncan didn't smile. He didn't feel embarrassed. He felt numb. The order was outrageous. Impossible.

"But how, John?" In the stunned silence, Ishbel's hands hovered above her work, unmoving. "How can ye catch more fish in less time? It canna' be done. Soon there will be no fish left for anybody."

"Aye. Truly, it canna' be done, my love." John Fisher looked down at his gnarled hands. The light from the cooking fire in the hearth reflected from the coins onto the moisture in the corner of his eyes. "Earning the coins doesn't matter," he said, looking from Ishbel and Fiona to Duncan, "but it wilna' be easy to break a promise to a King." He brushed a knuckle across his eye. "And, Duncan, lad, it would ha' been a fine thing to see ye appointed the Royal Fisher. A title ye could ha' passed on to your son, and he to his. Aye! An old man's folly, perhaps." He glanced up at his row of carved birds and fish and animals that paraded across the dark, wooden roof beams, then back to the block of wood in his hands. "There's little else in this poor life I ha' to give ye."

Duncan felt his mother's warmth as she moved close behind him. She cupped her hands on his shoulders. "You see, Duncan," she said, "we hoped that soon, perhaps, your father could turn the fishing over to you, and he could spend the rest of his days doing what he has always longed to do." Duncan's eyes had not left the form that was emerging from his father's white block – a swan with a long, curved neck reaching upward.

Something lodged in Duncan's throat. Even though he didn't enjoy fishing, even though he didn't want to be the Royal Fisher, tomorrow, he knew, he would fish as he had never fished before. He would do it, not for the King, but for his father. "Mother, the new net – is it finished?"

"Nearly." Ishbel Fisher crossed to a pile of knotted hemp.

"May I take it tomorrow?"

"To use from the bank?" The net fell from her hands. "It will be torn to pieces on rocks! Snagged on roots! Whatever are ye thinking? 'Tis impossible to use a net this large from the river's edge!"

"I'll be careful," Duncan promised, looking to his father. "I've got an idea."

John set the swan aside. Slowly, he reached for his pipe and carefully tamped tobacco into its bowl. "Perhaps, Ishbel, my love," he said, raising a bushy eyebrow over a twinkle of blue, "when facing the impossible, we must risk something new."

CHAPTER 9

Wearing only blue hose, Duncan slipped into the icy water of the stream. The new net slid smoothly through his hand. The weighted edge sank to the bottom as he pulled it across a quiet elbow of water that looped off from the swift current. He hoped the idea the otters had given him would succeed. Hope. That was all he was going on today: hope that his wild idea would work, hope that his father would net a good catch, hope that the Huntsman wouldn't come, and hope that the otters were as smart as he thought.

Duncan swung the gaff, but it look a long time even to hook four fish, one for each of the otters. "Chi!" he called. "Chi! Chirrp!"

Splash! Splash! Splash! Splash! The whole

otter family tumbled out of their holt and into the stream. "Chirp! Chirp!" They rolled and bobbed near where Duncan stood, as if they were inviting him to come in and play.

"No, not today." He picked up a stone and skipped it across the water. "The Huntsman wants your pelts. Unless you help me, he'll get them, and mine, too."

Like a pack of sheepdogs, the otter family bounded after the stone. Father Otter came back, carrying the prize. When Duncan said, "Give me the pebble," and clapped his hands, Father Otter set it on the bank. Duncan tossed the stone several more times, clapped, and said, "Bring me the pebble," and each time, someone did.

"Now let's see how smart you *really* are." Duncan dangled one of the fish he'd caught. "Fish," he said. "Fish. Bring me the fish!" He flung a salmon into the stream, and the four otters swam after it. Duncan clapped. Nosey scrambled out of the water with the fish and began to eat it, head first. "No!" Duncan clapped his hands. "Bring me the fish!" He held out his hand, and repeated, "Bring me the fish!" Nosey cocked her head and chewed away.

Duncan worked all morning, coaxing the otters. But they couldn't understand. They had eaten three of the four fish. This idea wasn't going to work. The otters simply didn't know what he was asking them to do. Overhead, the sun hovered in the middle of the sky. It was already midday. There was no more time to practice.

"All right, otters, fish!" he yelled. But this time he only pretended to throw. No fish sailed from his hand and there was no splash. "Fish!" he repeated. "Bring me a fish." He waited.

The otters waited, too, watching for the splash.

"Fish!" He knelt and clapped his hands. "Bring me a fish!" He waited.

The otters waited, too.

"Fish!"

Father Otter, Grilse, and Nosey watched, but finally, Mother Otter slid under the water. Her sleek body twisted and darted along the riverbed like a shadow, leaving a trail of bubbles. Before long, she returned. In her mouth she carried a thrashing salmon.

Duncan jumped up. "That's right, Mother Otter! Good! Good! You *do* understand! Bring it here." He clapped. "That's what I want you all to do."

Mother Otter dropped the fish and Duncan snatched it away. "Fish!" he cried. "Fish! All of you."

One by one, the otters caught on to the new game. Duncan was so excited he couldn't keep from shouting. "You'll show them, won't you? No one will want to make cloaks of you when they see what you can do." He danced along the edge of the grass, and leapt into the elbow of the stream behind the net.

"Fish! Fish! Bring me fish, lots of fish!" Clapping and prancing in the water, Duncan grabbed fish as the otters brought them and tossed them behind the net. "Four! Five! Six! Seven! It's a long way to two hundred and twenty-five, but oh, King! These fish will be fresh! Eight! Nine! Ten!" Almost faster than he could count, the otters brought fish to the edge of the net, gave them to him, then whisked around to fish for more. "Forty-three! Forty-four!" Duncan began to sing.

Otters, otters, fish for the King.

Otters, otters, fish for the Queen.

The dam behind the net became more and more full. Duncan wished his mother could see her new net now. Fish bumped against Duncan's legs and back, and still the otters brought more. Each trip took longer as they swam farther away. Duncan lost count. "Good, Grilse! Good for you!" he shouted, flipping a salmon over his shoulder. He glanced up at the sun. Wait until he told his father. Wait until he told Lillias. Nobody would want to kill otters ever again.

"Good, Father Otter! Good, Nosey. Nosey!" Suddenly, Nosey catapulted over the top of the net. "Hey! You're not supposed to be in here. This is for fish. Come on, Nosey! Get out of here." Laughing, he tried to catch her, but Nosey dived. He waited for her to surface, but she didn't surface, and the net began to thrash.

Duncan grabbed the net and pulled himself underwater. He tried to unhook the rough hemp from Nosey's flailing, webbed paws and legs, but she was frantic. The more he tried to help, the more she struggled, and the more she struggled, the more entangled she became. Duncan surfaced to breathe. The net tugged and pulled, but less violently now. Nosey's arms and legs slowed. Bubbles trailed up from her open mouth. With a jolt, Duncan realized that Nosey wasn't like a fish. She had to breathe the same way he did. Nosey was drowning.

He scrambled up the bank for his gutting knife, sliced through the middle section of net, and dragged Nosey up for air. Trailing the ragged edges of the net, he carried her to the stream bank.

Duncan lay Nosey on her back in the grass. Her feet and claws were still tangled in net. He pushed gently on her stomach. The light colored fur on her underbelly was wet and matted in clumps, like hair on a wet dog. Her pink tongue and droopy whiskers hung over her loose chin. A trickle of water ran from her mouth, down through the white fur on her throat.

The other three otters crept from the stream and circled around. They chirped and nudged Nosey with their noses. As Duncan pushed again, they suddenly fled. Nosey's leathery black paws twitched. Eyes still closed, she burped. Duncan sighed. "You're going to be all right, Nosey." Just then a sound made him look up and moan. "I'm not so sure about me, though."

Duncan's father was bearing down on him like

an angry bull.

"Father! How long…?"

"Och! Ye should ha' let the creature drown!" his father bellowed. He was out of breath, his face was flaming red, and he was trembling with anger. "Ye've ruined Mother's new net! Where is your catch?"

Duncan looked toward the ends of the net

trailing in the current. Only now did he realize what he had done. He'd let all the fish go free. "Gone."

"Gone!" John Fisher's voice echoed from the castle crag. "All gone? For an otter! And there are none in the Forth below the harbor. Fished out! Do you hear? No fish in the Forth! Now we have nothing for the King. Nothing!" His father's face held a fury Duncan had never seen before. "I tell ye, lad, we'll be rid of these pests once and for all! I'm going for the Huntsman!" He spun on his heel. Half-running, John Fisher headed back across the carseland toward Stirling.

CHAPTER 10

Duncan knew how Nosey felt underwater in the net. Panicked. Trapped.

Father would help the Huntsman. The Huntsman would help the Furrier. The Furrier would help the King. The King would give the Queen a new otter cloak for her birthday and a second cloak to someone named Lady Rebekah.

No one can help the otters except me. "Unless they change their minds," Duncan said aloud. "Nosey! We'll make them change their minds!" As fast as his cold fingers could move, he retied the torn net. Nosey grunted and growled, wrestling with the section of the net still tangled around her. "I'll help you! Just wait." Duncan replaced the mended net across the quiet backwater.

"Come back!" he yelled to Father, Mother, and Grilse. "Chichichichi! Fish! Fish! Fish! Fish! Come on, otters! Chi! Chi! Chi! Chichichichichi! Come on! We've got to do it again!"

When the otters came back, they didn't fish. They went straight to Nosey.

"Oh! All right!" Duncan exclaimed, realizing that they would never fish until Nosey was untangled. "But we've got to hurry!" His fingers unthreaded the net from around Nosey's paws so she could wiggle out. Then she rolled and squirmed until she was completely covered with dirt.

Duncan jumped into the backwater behind the net. "Now, fish! Fish! All of you! Fish!" He pretended to throw something out into the current. With a chorus of chirps, the otters slid down the bank. They bobbed a few times, then headed up the river.

Duncan knew that after their escape, the fish would have swum upriver as fast and as far as they could. They might have kept going all the way to the Allen Water and on to Dunblane.

Duncan sloshed up and down inside the net trap, getting colder and colder, waiting. Maybe the otters understood the danger and escaped into the mountains. Finally, he saw one, two, three, four heads, lilting along like driftwood across the water.

Not one carried a fish between its teeth.

"Ohhh, no." Weak-kneed, queasy in his stomach, and shivering, Duncan leaned against the net. An image of the Queen's otter cloak flitted before his eyes. Suddenly he jerked away. Underwater, one of the otters had bumped him. "But..." His eyes scanned the stream. All four were still out there, darting and diving back and forth in a semicircle in front of the net. Then the net began to shake and jounce and arch toward him, as alive as it had been when Nosey was trapped.

"Och! Aye!" Duncan shouted. Peering into the water, he could not believe what he saw. Fish! Dozens of fish. Dozens and dozens of fish. Hundreds of fish crowded together, trying to escape from the otters. "Nosey! Father Otter! You've herded the fish!" He shook his head in amazement, then realized what he must do. He grabbed the net.

"Ferniticles!"

Duncan jerked around to see Myron standing on firm, dry land at the edge of the marsh. Myron was

shouting and pointing toward the otters.

"What are those?" His voice had to carry a very long way. "What are they doing? What are you doing? The King is very angry. Yesterday's fish were not fresh!"

"Myron! That's not important now. Myron, please. You must run and ask the King to come!"

"Ask the King! To come? Here?" Myron's mouth dropped open like a trapdoor on a loose hinge.

"Yes!" Duncan struggled to climb the slippery bank, still urging the otters. "Fish! Fish! Fish! Good, Mother Otter! Good, Father! I'll get this net lowered in a minute! Don't let them get away!" He called to Myron. "Please, Myron. Don't come any closer. They'll smell you and run away. You must fetch the King." His fingers fumbled with the knots. "Tell the King that if he comes, I promise him the freshest fish in the world. Forever!"

Even from this distance, Myron looked confused. "Nobody ever sends for the King! Nobody ever runs from the King, either. But the King does find you interesting, Fernitickles. Perhaps he'll come."

"He must come! Hurry!" Duncan splashed back into the water with the slack net in his hand. The net rippled like a long, white wave, then sank. Before the onslaught of herding otters, fish zipped across the net, bumping Duncan's cold legs.

Glancing up, Duncan saw Myron's horse standing patiently, tied to a patch of wild raspberries. The tip of the feather atop Myron's flat hat was jouncing along the path, back toward the castle.

"Oh, please come, King!" Duncan said out loud. "You must come! And hurry! Only you can stop the Huntsman."

CHAPTER 11

Duncan tugged the net back into place, a fence between the otters and salmon. Even more fish were trapped this time. They were so crowded, their fins stuck above the water. Duncan's spirit soared. Nobody – not his father, not the Huntsman, not the King himself – could possibly want the otters' pelts now. Happily, he piped back at the plovers that were poking their long bills into the muddy bank. Then he began a little ditty he made up as he sang.

> Otters, otters, fish for the King.
> Otters, otters, fish for the Queen.
> You won't be a cloak for the Queen,
> When they see you fish for the King.
> Otters, otters...

His song was interrupted by shouting.

"There!" His father and the Huntsman rushed toward the river. "There they are! Shoot! Shoot them all before they get away!"

Swiftly, the Huntsman slid the crossbow and arrow from his back and took aim.

"No!" Duncan threw himself between the Huntsman's arrow and the fleeing otters. "You canna' shoot the otters! Look, Father! Look at the fish! Dozens of fish! Hundreds of fish! The otters caught them for us!"

John Fisher stared at the water. His mustache and eyebrows moved, but no words came from his mouth. Without taking his eyes from the fins, he raised his hand and pulled down the Huntsman's crossbow. His pipe swiveled upside down. Tobacco sprinkled over his tunic. In a daze, he walked toward the stream. When he reached the edge, he kept walking, right into the water, right into the mass of writhing fish. "'Tis a miracle, son! A miracle!" His voice wobbled like a spent top.

Duncan laughed. "It's no miracle! It's the otters! They're the best fishers of all. With their help, the King will always eat fresh fish!"

By the raspberry bush, Myron's horse nickered and pointed its ears toward the woods. Duncan, his father, and the Huntsman all turned as Myron's feather waved into sight. Three mounted guards followed Myron, each carrying a spear. After the guards, the King!

King James rode a brown and white horse, and a brown and white hunting dog trotted at his side. When the King's eyes found him, Duncan shivered just as he had before. He stood as respectfully as he could in water above his waist.

Beside him, a strange sound gurgled in his father's throat. Duncan glanced and saw Father's eyebrows shoot up high and vanish beneath his shock of white hair. Then his father bowed so quickly and so low that his face and pipe splatted right into the river.

"You sent for me?" The King's voice boomed. He was looking directly at Duncan.

"Yy – ee – ss, Your Majesty, Sir." Duncan's voice squeaked out, a mere whisper.

The King glanced to his left. "This isn't another trap, is it? You are not planning to kidnap me, are you?" The King glanced to his right. "The way they did when I was out hunting at Royston?"

"Oh, no! No, Your Majesty!" Duncan couldn't tell. Was the King joking? He didn't seem to be joking. He seemed a little scared. "I would *never* do that!"

"Nobody is going to try to blow me up the way Guy Fawkes did?"

"Oh, no! No, Your Majesty! I wouldn't dream of doing that, either!"

"Or steal Mr. Jowler?" Duncan glanced at the dog that was sitting on its haunches beside the King's horse.

"Oh, no, Your Majesty. No one will take your dog."

"Well, at Royston someone did. They kept him all night, then sent him back with a message tied around his neck. It said…" The King frowned. "What did it say, Myron?"

Myron stretched himself tall. "Your Majesty, it said:

'Good Mr. Jowler,

We pray you speak to the King (for he hears you every day, and so doth not us) that it will please His Majesty to go back to London, or else the country will be undone; all our provision is spent already and we are unable to entertain him any longer.'"

"Ach!" Duncan choked back a laugh. So Stirling isn't the only place to suffer from feeding the King and his court! "Oh, I wouldn't do that, either, Your Majesty. I canna' write."

"Hummm." The King stroked his beard and looked straight at Duncan's nose. "What an awful lot of freckles you have, Fernitickles. Fernitickles, aren't you the boy who ran from me, the King?"

Duncan took a deep breath and nodded.

"May I ask why?" The King's voice rolled up and down, like low music.

"I – I wasn't really running *from* you, Your Majesty, Sir," Duncan stammered. "I was running *to* something else."

"And what, pray tell, would that have been?"

From the corner of his eye, Duncan could see his father's head turning back and forth, watching him and the King as if he were watching a ball game. "Otters," Duncan answered.

"Otters?" the King exclaimed.

"Yes, Your Majesty, Sir," Duncan said. "Otters."

"Am I to understand that you would rather be in the marsh with otters than with your King?"

Duncan lowered his eyes. "Yes, Sir."

Suddenly the carseland boomed with sound. It bounced and catapulted from the Forth Valley to the castle crag, louder than the bugle of a cornet. The King was laughing.

"Well, Duncan Fisher, son of John Fisher, Fisher of the Royal Burgh of Stirling…" The King struggled to bring himself under control, wiping the corner of his eye with a white lace handkerchief. "Why have you sent for me?"

The King's laughter had made Duncan want to laugh, too, but his knees were quivering in the icy water. He thought fast. The lives of his otters depended on his answer.

"B – because you are a good King – wise and slow to anger. And, and because you like your fish fresh." Duncan pointed to the churning fins behind the net. "I'm sorry not all of the fish were fresh yesterday. But see these fish? They couldn't be fresher. They're still alive! The otters caught them for you."

"Otters?" the King exclaimed for the second time. "What otters?" He peered at the river.

"Yes," Duncan rushed on, "otters. But, Your Majesty, Sir, you ordered a cloak for the birthday of the Queen, and another cloak for someone else. The Huntsman wants to kill the otters for their pelts."

"Indeed!" The King looked at the Huntsman, then back to Duncan. "Well, where are these otters? I want to see them."

"Begging your pardon, Sir, but I think they're hiding. I think your laugh… I think we frightened them away. But if you would like to hide behind that raspberry bush and be very still for a while…"

Like the boom of a great drum, the King's laughter resonated again. Startled, a long-legged heron rose into the air, beating its wings. "Very well, young man. The King shall hide. I suppose young lads do things like that. I wouldn't know. When I was a lad, I was kept like a prisoner in that castle there. So now, that castle and the royal guests can wait. Young Duncan Fisher, I find you and these otters of yours much more entertaining than they." He looked around the marshy land along the river. "Where would you have us hide?"

"Up there would be fine." Duncan pointed to the raspberry bushes near Myron's horse. "May my father go with you?"

With water dripping from his hair and clothes, Duncan's father waded from the stream and sloshed along behind the King, Myron the Messenger, the Huntsman, and the King's guards. Then, like children playing, they all hid behind the raspberry bush.

Duncan quickly crawled from the stream and slipped into his clothes. He hoped his mending would hold the bulging net a while longer. He sat by the stream and dangled his fingers in the water.

Knowing the King was watching made time seem to go on forever, but Duncan wanted the otters to feel safe, so he waited. And he worried. What if, this time, the otters wouldn't come? What if they wouldn't fish? What if the King wasn't able to see what they could do? He shook the thoughts from his head. Finally, when the carseland sounded normal again, he called. "Chi! Chichichichichi! Chi! Chichichichichi!"

A dark shadow slipped from the otter holt into the river. Noiselessly, it swam through the water to Duncan's hand.

Duncan wiggled his fingers. "Just you, Father Otter?" The rest of the family was nowhere in sight.

"Well, this is it, our last chance. We'd better do it right." Duncan looked around. He dug Nosey's tooth-marked golf ball from his leather bag, held it up for Father Otter – and the King – to see, and tossed it from hand to hand.

Father Otter rolled over onto his back, holding his paws together as if he were praying. His dark eyes sparkled.

"Bring me the golf ball, Father Otter!" Duncan shouted as he hoisted the ball into the stream.

Father Otter swiveled, dived, poked the golf ball with his nose, nudged it harder, and bumped it up into the air. Then, like a kitten, he tackled the ball and pulled it underwater. Duncan couldn't help laughing, in spite of the King. When Father Otter finally returned the ball, Duncan said, "Now, fish! Fish, Father Otter, as if your life depended on it! Because it does!"

Father Otter dived. Duncan watched him dart like a black shadow against the current. He veered one direction, then another, then abruptly turned and swam, straight as an arrow, back to Duncan. A plump salmon wiggled from his mouth. Duncan held the salmon high for the King to see.

"Amazing!" The King rose up from behind the bush, nearly losing his balance. "Amazing!"

With a flip of his tail and a startled peep, Father Otter vanished.

"When all the otters were here," Duncan called, "they herded the fish, like shepherds driving sheep. There are four of them. Father and Mother and two young cubs, Nosey and Grilse." He gestured to the net. "See?" Somehow the King didn't seem so scary once Duncan had seen him hiding in the bushes. "So, Your Majesty, Sir, you wouldn't want the Huntsman to kill them," Duncan said, searching the King's face, "for a cloak for the Queen." When the King still didn't answer, he added meekly, "Would you?"

The King stretched himself to his full height. "I

shall return to the castle to attend to my guests. Stay here, Myron, and deliver the fish when they're ready. Thank goodness," the King sighed, "those pesky guests leave in the morn. One last boring royal banquet and they'll all be gone." He groaned and cast a glance back at Duncan. "Be thankful you are not a King, lad. I'd much rather have been a scholar. Maybe even a fisher, like you."

Duncan breathed a little easier. At least the huge orders would stop, but the King hadn't answered his question. "But, Your Majesty, Sir," Duncan interjected, "the otters?"

The King collected his horse, then turned abruptly. "I command you, Fernitickles Fisher, along with you, John Fisher, Fisher of the Royal Burgh of Stirling, to await my decision tomorrow midday at the Mercat Cross on Broad Street." He looked at the Huntsman. "And, you, Huntsman. You be there, too."

Duncan swallowed hard as he bowed. Why wait until tomorrow to decide? Didn't the King see that the otters should live? Couldn't he say so right now? Speechless, Duncan watched the King ride away.

CHAPTER 12

All the following morning, small parties of departing royal guests wound their way through the town of Stirling. The townspeople, including Duncan and his family, watched from outside their cottages and shops. Stories sped up and down the street, mouth to ear, mouth to ear, from one onlooker to another.

"That man's a duke! She a duchess!

"Duke and duchess!"

"Duke and duchess!"

"There's the Earl of Mar."

"The Earl of Mar."

"The Earl of Mar."

"The Countess of Argyll."

"The Countess of Argyll."

The stories of Duncan's encounter with the King passed, too, like red flags in a relay.

"And did ye hear? Late last night the King sent for Tom the Tinker, and he hasn't yet returned."

"Tom the Tinker hasn't returned."

"Tom the Tinker."

"The Tinker hasn't returned."

Duncan paced out into the cobblestone street to check the position of the sun. The King had said "midday."

Fiona tagged along after him, carrying a slate and piece of chalky rock in her hand. "Is this the way Nosey looked?"

In spite of his worry, Duncan had to laugh at Fiona's drawing of Nosey tangled in the net. It looked like a blob with a nose and a mass of crisscrossed lines. "Exactly!" he said.

John Fisher squinted up from the tiny slivers of wood that were becoming an otter's whiskers under his touch. He looked at his daughter's drawing and chuckled. "Fiona, how did that brother of yours ever teach those creatures to mind?"

"They're smart!" Fiona said, then sang the song that Duncan had taught her.

Otters, otters, fish for the King.

Otters, otters, fish for the Queen.

You won't be a cloak for the Queen,

When they see you fish for the King.

"Father! If the King saves the otters, the otters can fish for you. And you can carve all the time. You can finish the nativity set and Mother's goblets, and my new doll, and..."

For a moment the click! click! click! of knitting needles stopped and Duncan's mother let the heavy winter shawl she was making rest on her lap. "Now wouldn't that be bonny?" Duncan saw her dreamy smile shift to his father. She said, "Otters are smart, as smart as they are fun. When I was a wee lassie, I watched them, too." She nodded at Duncan. "Dinna' fret, son. If our King is a good King and wise, he will make the right decision."

"I hope so, Mother. But if he's so wise, why didn't he decide yesterday?"

Ishbel's needles began to click again. "Perhaps it takes important people a longer time to think."

Finally, so many royal guests had passed that Duncan thought the castle must be nearly empty. The sun glared directly overhead. "It's time,"

Duncan said, unable to stand still.

"Yes, 'tis the time." John Fisher set his three-legged stool and the nearly finished wooden otter aside. "May good fortune shine. No matter what happens, I'm proud of ye, son. I certainly was wrong about those otters," he muttered, shaking his head.

"Father," Duncan said, "maybe I was wrong about the King. A little, anyway."

Together, Duncan, John, Ishbel, and Fiona walked down the cobblestone street to meet the King. The Shoemaker's family joined them as they passed by. "What do ye think the King will say?" the Shoemaker asked.

"Dinna ken," John Fisher grumbled.

As they walked into the spicy aroma surrounding the bakery, the Baxter's family fell into step beside them. "How do ye think the King will decide?" the Baxter asked.

"For the otters, Father! Of course!" Lillias squeezed in beside Duncan, smiling. "I know he will, Duncan! He has to!"

Charles Fisher rushed out from the fenced pasture behind his cheese shop, where milk cows were mooing and goats were bleating. "Well, nephew," he said, slapping a big hand on Duncan's shoulder, "I hope the King will change his mind about a cloak for the Queen."

Duncan nodded. "So do I."

By the time they reached Janet Kilbowie's tavern, all the townspeople had circled around, and everyone was talking.

"How did ye do it, Duncan? How did ye train wild otters to fish?"

"'Tis true ye asked the King to come?"

"Did the King hide behind a raspberry bush and muddy his knees?"

Everybody was asking questions, but nobody was giving Duncan a chance to answer. Duncan saw the Huntsman and the Furrier standing on the fringe of the crowd, smiling. At the corner of St. Mary's Wynd, Uncle William and his band of friends stood apart, watching. A belt of fear wrapped around Duncan's stomach, then squeezed when someone shouted, "Here comes the King!"

Like tall grass in the wind, the townspeople bowed low. Duncan bowed even deeper and lower than the rest. He felt the power of the King's eyes and began to tremble.

The King, the Royal Page, the Royal Guards, and Myron the Messenger approached. Behind them, toting a bag and looking quite important, trailed Tom the Tinker.

The King took his position in the middle of Broad Street, where public proclamations – and judgments – were made. Guards flanked either side. The Royal Page stepped forward. "Hear Ye! Hear Ye!" the Page cried, stiffly holding a parchment scroll in front of him. "All ye burgesses and citizens of the Royal Burgh of Stirling, hear the proclamation of the King."

With great pomp, the Page removed a red ribbon from the scroll. He broke the King's wax seal, unrolled the scroll, and began to read. "Inasmuch as the King is the King of all of the land, and inasmuch as all of the land falls under the dominion of the King, and inasmuch as the wild creatures of the forest are a part of the land and therefore fall under the dominion of the King, and inasmuch as wild otters are wild creatures of the forest that are part of the land that falls under the dominion of the King, and as the fish of the rivers are part of the land that falls under the dominion of the King, and inasmuch as the otters of the land fish the fish of the rivers and the King likes fresh fish…"

Duncan had understood very little so far, but now the Page paused as if he finally had something important to say. "The King hereby appoints Fernitickles Fisher, son of John Fisher, Fisher of the Royal Burgh of Stirling…" He paused again. "KEEPER OF THE KING'S OTTERS!"

Whispers of exclamation rippled through the crowd.

"Keeper of the King's Otters!"

"A royal post!"

"An appointment from the King!"

"The first royal appointment in Stirling!"

Duncan felt dizzy. What did it mean? Why couldn't the King just tell the Huntsman not to kill otters? Why couldn't the Page speak in a simple way?

"From this day forward," the Page read on, "to watch over and protect the otters of the Water of the Forth at Stirling, to exact from the otters fresh fish at his royal command, to…"

"Enough of this balderdash!" The King's voice

raised over the crowd. His face was beaming. He was practically dancing, though unsteadily, on the tips of his toes. He brushed the Page away, and impatiently wagged a jeweled index finger toward Tom the Tinker. "Come here."

With an air of great importance, Tom the Tinker strode to the King's side.

"Open it, Tinker. Open the bag." Reaching inside, the King pulled out a large metal disk with an otter etched in the middle. Around the otter marched a ring of strange symbols. He held it up for the people to see.

"Step up, Fernitickles of the Royal Burgh of Stirling," the King said in a strong voice. His eyes were twinkling. "Well, come up here, Fernitickles. Don't be backward."

Duncan's feet felt as if they were planted in mud. He pulled them up, one after the other. He was shaking at the knees. The King smiled down on him. Duncan lowered his eyes, then felt the King slip a thin silk band over his head. "I hereby appoint you, Fernitickles…?" The King tipped his head to one side, listening to his own voice. "That can't be your real name, can it, lad?"

"No, Your Majesty, Sir. My name is Duncan Fisher."

"I hereby appoint you, Duncan Fisher, to the royal post of 'Keeper of the King's Otters.' An honorary title," the King coughed lightly, adding in an undertone, "without pay."

Duncan stared down at the shining disk on his chest. "Y–you mean the Huntsman canna' take the otters' pelts?"

"Of course not!" The King's laughter echoed from Broad Street to St. Mary's Wynd. "Not after the way you've trained them."

"I – I won't be the Fisher of Stirling like my father?"

"Well-llll," the King fudged, "you will bring my fish when I am here. But your title, and that of your sons and their sons, and... who knows?" He laughed a little chuckle of delight. "Maybe their daughters, too, shall be 'Keeper of the King's Otters'."

"You mean I'll be able to spend my whole life watching otters?"

"Yes, young Duncan Fisher, that's exactly what I mean!"

Duncan stared at the King. He turned to the smiling faces of his family and Lillias, then back to the King. All the crowd, even the Furrier and the Huntsman, began to laugh, and finally Duncan understood. He leapt into the air and when he landed, his great metal badge of honor thumped hard against his chest.

"Thank you! Thank you, Your Majesty!" He bowed to the King, once, twice, three times. "Thank you!" Everyone was laughing, but Duncan didn't care. "You really *are* a wise King! And I will take good care of your otters! There's nothing in the whole world I would rather do!" Duncan's spinning head spun out another thought. "And if the King's otters could fish for the town, too, then my father could spend his time carving."

The King laughed again. "Of course! Of course! The otters will fish for everyone!"

"And nobody will hunt them? Ever again?" Duncan craned his neck to see the Huntsman at the back of the crowd.

"Absolutely not." The King sighed. "Oh, I do love to hunt, but when I kill, it makes me sad." The King's face wrinkled; his eyebrows pulled together.

"I shall have to think of something else for the Queen's birthday, and for a gift for this Indian Princess from America who will be arriving soon as the Queen's guest. What is her name, Myron?

"Lady Rebekah, Sir. The wife of colonist Thomas Rolfe."

"Yes, I know that! But what is her real name?"

"Pocahontas, Your Majesty."

"Pocahontas? Yes, that's it! I must have gifts for both of them."

"Excuse me, Sir." The sweet, soft voice of Duncan's little sister, Fiona, wafted forward from the front edge of the crowd. Everyone quieted. Fiona curtsied low, then a rush of excited words escaped. "Mother makes Duncan and me warm clothes from the wool the sheep don't need anymore when it gets hot. The sheep don't have to die. Nothing has to die." Her big, baby blue eyes were wide and trusting. "Our mother could knit a warm cloak for your Queen. And for the Indian Princess, too."

Duncan's chest felt full, as if it were going to burst. He glanced from his little sister to the proud faces of his parents. He knew, for the first time, exactly how his father and mother felt. He had never been so proud in his life.

The King's face twitched, then worked its way into a crooked smile. His hand dug into his lace sleeve for a handkerchief. He dabbed the corner of his eye. "What a noble idea, little girl! What a noble idea! From the mouths of children..." His words trailed off. His eyes raised to Duncan's mother. "Would you, ma'am?"

Ishbel curtsied low. "I would be honored, Your Majesty," she answered simply.

"Duncan Fisher, you are fortunate to have such a mother." The King looked wistfully toward the castle. "I never saw my mother after I was a baby. Not once when I was a youth or in all those years she was in prison before her beheading."

The King rose to his full height. "But what is past is past." He shook his head, then, smiling at Duncan, he said, "Now, Keeper of the King's Otters, bring a dozen fresh Stirling salmon to the castle for my royal dinner."

"Yes, Sir, Your Majesty!" Duncan bowed, but this time he was smiling, too. Even though he felt the King's eyes on him, he didn't tremble. "Thank you. Thank you, Your Majesty."

Duncan darted away, then, on an impulse, turned back to Lillias. "Would you like to come, too?"

Together, hand in hand, Lillias and Duncan ran down Broad Street, to St. Mary's Wynd, and down the steep road toward Stirling Bridge. Where the Water of Forth meandered through the boggy carseland, they left the old Roman causeway and followed a narrow, muddy path along the winding river.

"Chi!" Duncan called. "Chi! Chichichichi!"

Glossary

bannock – a thin, flat oatmeal or barley biscuit

brig – a small jail

carseland – wet, marshy grasslands

cobbler – someone who makes shoes and boots

conies – rabbits

cornet – a small brass instrument like a trumpet

crag – a steep, rugged rock or cliff

crown – the highest part of a hill or a road

dinna ken – do not know

ditty – a simple song

dolerite – a dark gray or black coarse rock

gaff – a handled hook for holding or lifting heavy fish

Guy Fawkes – the leader of a plot in England to blow up King James I and Parliament in 1606

ha' – shortened version of "have" in common speech

holt – otters' lair

Och! Aye! – a Scottish exclamation that became the expression "OK" used today

plover – a shorebird that uses its short, hard beak to dig insects and crabs for food

promontory – a high point of land or rock overlooking a low plain or a body of water

scat – animal droppings

tinker – someone who mends or creates household utensils and works with metals

tron – a big, built-in scale used to weigh goods

whilst – while

ye – you

Bibliography

Extracts from the Records of the Royal Burgh of Sterling A.D. 1519-1666, Ed. R. Renwick, 1887.

Geographic Guide – Northern Scotland, Tripp.

History of England, S. E. Gardiner, Vols. 1, 2, 3, 4, 5. AMS Press, New York, 1965.

The Intelligent Traveller's Guide to Historic Scotland, Philip A. Crowl, Congdon and Weed, New York, 1986.

James I, Otto J. Scott, Mason/Charter, New York, 1976.

The Reign of James VI and I, Ed. Alan G. R. Smith. St. Martin's Press, New York, 1973.

Shearer's Illustrated Guide, Sterling and Neighborhood, R. S. Shearer, Sterling, 1883.

Sterling, the Royal Burgh, Craig Mair, John Donald Publishers, Edinburgh, 1990.

The Track of the Wild Otters, Hugh Miles, Colin Barter Photography, Ltd., 1989.

A *Vertebrate Fauna of Forth*, Oliver and Boyd, Edinburgh: Tivesdale Court, London, 1935.

TITLES IN THE SERIES

SET 9A

Television Drama
Time for Sale
The Shady Deal
The Loch Ness Monster Mystery
Secrets of the Desert

SET 9B

To JJ From CC
Pandora's Box
The Birthday Disaster
The Song of the Mantis
Helping the Hoiho

SET 9C

Glumly
Rupert and the Griffin
The Tree, the Trunk, and the Tuba
Errol the Peril
Cassidy's Magic

SET 9D

Barney
Get a Grip, Pip!
Casey's Case
Dear Future
Strange Meetings

SET 10A

A Battle of Words
The Rainbow Solution
Fortune's Friend
Eureka
It's a Frog's Life

SET 10B

The Cat Burglar of Pethaven Drive
The Matchbox
In Search of the Great Bears
Many Happy Returns
Spider Relatives

SET 10C

Horrible Hank
Brian's Brilliant Career
Fernitickles
It's All in Your Mind,
    James Robert
Wing High, Gooftah

SET 10D

The Week of the Jellyhoppers
Timothy Whuffenpuffen-
    Whippersnapper
Timedetectors
Ryan's Dog Ringo
The Secret of Kiribu Tapu Lagoon